Copycat

Story by Joy Cowley
Illustrations by Murray Grimsdale

I go up the path.
You go up the path.

2

I go up the steps.
You go up the steps.

3

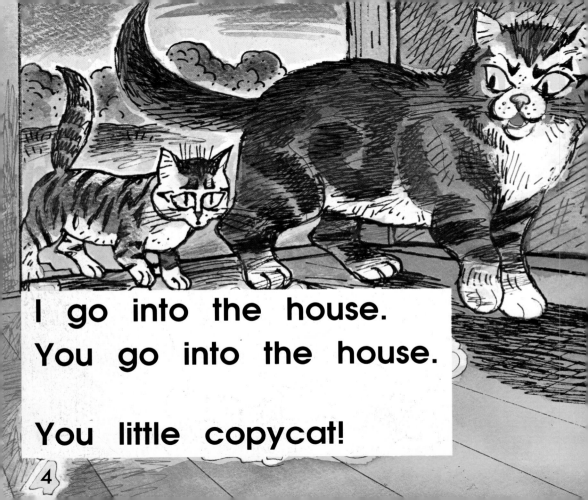

I go into the house.
You go into the house.

You little copycat!

4

I go down the steps.
You go down the steps.

6

I go down the path.
You go down the path.

I go up the tree.
You go up the tree.

You big copycat!

8